Nicolaus Copernicus

THE EARTH IS A PLANET

BY DENNIS BRINDELL FRADIN

ILLUSTRATED BY CYNTHIA VON BUHLER

MONDO

NEW YORK

To the memory of my grandfather,
Louis Brindel,
who taught me to love astronomy

D. B. F.

2

For aural astronaut Adam Buhler,

and for my father,

Louis Carrozza,

who made his six children recite the planets in

order before we went to bed at night.

C. V. B.

3

*H*igh up in a cathedral tower, a man in a long robe gazes at the night sky. The time is the early 1500s—a century before the invention of the telescope. The man does have a few instruments, however. He measures star and planet positions with devices that look like several wooden yardsticks joined together. He also has a simple metal tube through which he views portions of the sky.

One heavenly body especially intrigues the man. Unlike the stars, it does not twinkle. Instead, it shines with a steady reddish glow, for it is the planet Mars. The man has viewed Mars on many nights over the years. All that time, something about the red planet's motion has puzzled him. Sometimes while wandering through the constellations, Mars makes a backward loop before continuing on its way. For centuries, these odd movements have mystified astronomers.

Perhaps the man is gazing at the sky one night when he thinks of the answer. Memories from his childhood help him find the solution. The man's name is Nicolaus Copernicus. In time, he will challenge the way people have viewed the Universe for ages.

Nicolaus was born on February 19, 1473, in Torun, Poland. His last name wasn't yet Copernicus, though. It was Koppernigk, sometimes also written Copernik in an age when little attention was paid to spelling.

Nicolaus was the youngest of four children. His father was a merchant and banker. The family owned a large home in Torun and a summerhouse near the grape fields outside town.

During the winter, young Nicolaus and his sisters and brother skated on the frozen Vistula River. During the summer, they played tag and ran races. Nicolaus learned to ride a horse and traveled with his family by wagon. A keen observer, he noticed something while running and riding. To a person moving fast, someone moving more slowly can appear to be going backward. Years later, this everyday observation would help him make a great discovery.

Nicolaus was only ten when his father died. His mother also died around then. Her brother Lucas, a clergyman who later became a bishop, adopted Nicolaus, his brother, and their two sisters. Uncle Lucas was so stern that people claimed he was never seen to laugh. But he raised his sister's four children and made sure that they became something in the world.

Uncle Lucas decided that Nicolaus, who was quiet and thoughtful, should become a clergyman like himself. He enrolled Nicolaus at the Cathedral School at Wloclawek, Poland, 40 miles from Torun. At this school, Nicolaus reportedly helped a teacher named Abstemius build a sundial for Wloclawek Cathedral. A sundial keeps track of time. It does this by measuring the changing angle of a shadow cast by the Sun as it crosses the sky. Perhaps building this sundial first interested Nicolaus in astronomy—the study of stars, planets, and other heavenly bodies.

When Nicolaus was 18, his uncle sent him to the university in Krakow, Poland. In those days, scholars often took on fancy names. The youth from Torun changed his name to Copernicus. Nic, as he sometimes signed his name, loved school. He attended colleges in Poland and Italy until he was 33 years old. He studied Latin, canon law (church law), and medicine. But his favorite subject was astronomy.

His astronomy professors taught Nicolaus many things that were later proved to be wrong.

Students of Nicolaus's day were taught that the Earth was a special body at the center of the Universe that stood motionless while all the heavenly bodies circled it. People had believed this since ancient times. Astronomy teachers had many arguments to support this idea.

It was impossible for the Earth to move, they said. Wouldn't we feel dizzy if the Earth was spinning or moving through space? Wouldn't we be thrown off the Earth's surface? Wouldn't a ball tossed into the sky be left behind and land miles away? Wouldn't clouds and birds also be left behind if the Earth moved?

Besides, anyone could see that the heavenly bodies circled the Earth. Each morning the Sun rose in the east. It traveled across the sky all day before setting in the west. At night the Moon and stars also crossed the sky, as did the five known planets—Mercury, Venus, Mars, Jupiter, and Saturn. The backward loops Mars and other planets sometimes made puzzled astronomers. Still, they saw no reason to doubt the age-old idea that the Earth was the center of the Universe.

In his studies, Nicolaus read about an ancient Greek astronomer named Aristarchus. The heavenly bodies don't really circle the Earth, Aristarchus had claimed. They only seem to do this because the Earth spins. Besides spinning, the Earth also travels around the Sun, Aristarchus added. For holding such strange ideas, Aristarchus was believed to have lost his mind.

Nicolaus thought about what his teachers said and about what the "crackpot" Aristarchus had claimed. While reading his books, Nicolaus made notes in the margins as ideas came to him. When no paper was available, he wrote down his ideas on calendars or even on walls! His notes show that, by age 20, he was starting to think that the "crazy" Aristarchus had been right.

Bog pomagay

16

Nicolaus finally finished college in 1506. He spent the rest of his life working as a clergyman and physician. Most of the time he was stationed at Poland's Frauenburg Cathedral near the Baltic Sea.

The cathedral resembled a castle. For his living space, Nicolaus chose a tower with an open view of the sky. His church duties included conducting services, collecting taxes, and overseeing lands. As a physician, he became known for treating the local poor people. In the early 1500s, doctors knew little about disease. A medical book still exists in which Copernicus wrote *Bog pomagay*. He must have felt hopeless about treating a patient, for those words mean "God help" in Polish.

At the end of his day's work, he observed the heavens from his tower. One of his observations was dated June 5, 1512. That night he observed Mars, which was in the midst of one of its backward loops. As usual, he wondered: Why does the red planet do that? Perhaps he was gazing at Mars when the answer came to him.

There was a logical reason for the red planet's backward loops, Copernicus realized. He recalled his childhood observation that a slow moving object can appear to go backward from the vantage point of a passing faster object. Wouldn't the same thing be true of planets?

19

Earth must not be standing still at the center of the Universe as everyone believed. Instead, it and the other planets orbit the Sun, like the "crackpot" Aristarchus had said. Earth is closer to the Sun than Mars and moves faster than the red planet. At times, Earth overtakes and passes Mars as both planets orbit the Sun. At those times, Mars appears to make a backward loop in the sky for a few months.

Once he realized that Earth was a planet orbiting the Sun, everything fell into place. Why do all the heavenly bodies seem to circle above us? For the same reason an ice-skater doing a spin can have the illusion that everything is spinning around him. The stars only *appear* to cross the sky from east to west each night because the Earth is spinning. For the same reason, the Sun only *appears* to cross the sky each day.

21

If the Earth spins like a top and orbits the Sun, why don't we feel the motion or get thrown into space? Because the Earth is huge and moves smoothly. Why don't clouds, birds, or a ball tossed in the air get left behind as the Earth moves? Because the air surrounding the Earth moves along with it.

Around 1512, Copernicus wrote a booklet stating that the Earth is a planet orbiting the Sun. He called it *Little Commentary*. As a Catholic clergyman, he had to be cautious. The Church insisted that the Earth was the center of the Universe. A clergyman who disputed this could be punished. So instead of having his booklet printed in large numbers, he just wrote several copies by hand and showed them to a few friends.

Upon completing *Little Commentary*, Nicolaus began a much longer work. Night after night, he viewed the heavens from his tower and worked on his book. For 30 years, he wrote and rewrote his great work. He wanted to publish it, but kept delaying for fear of punishment by the Church. By 1541, he was 68 years old. That was considered quite elderly at the time. Besides, Copernicus was suffering from a serious heart condition. Realizing that it would be wrong for his ideas to die with him, he unlocked the drawer where he kept his manuscript. At long last, he sent it to a publisher.

By then, he was so ill it appeared he would not live to see his book come off the press. But he clung to life until May 24, 1543. On that day a messenger rushed to his bedside with the first printed copy. He held his book in his hands. Within a few hours, he died at the age of 70 in the tower where he had spent much of his life.

Copernicus's masterpiece, *Concerning the Revolutions of the Heavenly Spheres,* was one of the most important books ever written. It offered the best arguments that had ever been made that the Earth is a planet. In a famous passage, he wrote that the planets revolve around the Sun. He continued:

How could this light be given a better place to illuminate the whole temple of God? . . . Let it in truth guide the circling family of planets, including the Earth. What a picture—so simple, so clear, so beautiful.

At first Copernicus's great book changed few minds. People were slow to let go of the idea that the Earth was the center of everything. Religious leaders especially opposed what came to be called the Copernican System: the idea that the Earth spins and orbits the Sun with other planets. In the year 1600, the Italian scholar Giordano Bruno was burned to death in Rome, partly for teaching Copernicus's ideas.

But the truth couldn't be held back forever. Little by little, proof of the Copernican system was found. In the winter of 1609-1610, Galileo Galilei of Italy became the first scientist to make astronomical discoveries with a telescope. While viewing Jupiter, Galileo saw four moons orbiting the giant planet. Here was proof that at least some heavenly bodies didn't orbit the Earth.

Then in 1687, the English scientist Isaac Newton published a book describing how the Sun's gravitation holds the planets in their orbits. Newton's book finally convinced the world that Copernicus had been right: the Earth spins and orbits the Sun. When asked about his achievements, Newton made a famous comment. "If I have seen further than others," he said, "it was because I stood upon the shoulders of giants." Newton meant that he had built on the work of Copernicus and other early astronomers. The same could be said of Copernicus, who had enlarged upon the work of Aristarchus.

In the mid-1900s, astronauts in space *saw* that the Earth spins and moves around the Sun. Then in the 1990s, there was a great new break-through. Astronomers discovered that, like the Sun, other stars are orbited by planets. These astronomers, too, have stood on the shoulders of a giant, Nicolaus Copernicus.

Author's Note

I have been fascinated by Nicolaus Copernicus since childhood when my grandfather took me to Chicago's Adler Planetarium and told me about the great astronomers. Recently while writing other astronomy books, I was startled to find that there is not much material in English about Copernicus. I had to piece together information for this book from many sources. A book I used 40 years ago in college, *The World of Copernicus* by Angus Armitage (Signet, 1963), was most helpful. Also of great help were *Messiah of Science Kopernik* by Arthur Waldo (Kopernik Quinquecentennial Committee of Arizona, 1947), *Nicholas Copernicus* by Stephen Mizwa (Kosciuszko Foundation, 1943), and *And There Was Light* by Rudolf Thiel (Knopf, 1957). Richard Talcott of *Astronomy* magazine answered some of my questions about the planets.

D. B. F.

Grateful acknowledgment is made to James Lattimer, of the Department of Physics and Astronomy at the State University of New York at Stony Brook, for vetting the scientific material in this book for accuracy.

For information contact:
MONDO Publishing
980 Avenue of the Americas
New York, NY 10018
Visit our web site at http://www.mondopub.com

Printed in China
03 04 05 06 07 08 09 HC 9 8 7 6 5 4 3 2 1
03 04 05 06 07 08 09 PB 9 8 7 6 5 4 3 2 1

ISBN   1-59336-006-1 (hc)   1-59336-007-x (pb)

Designed by E. Friedman
Cynthia von Buhler created the artwork for this book
using oil paint on gesso-textured paper, then scratching into the surface with a blade,
and applying gold leaf borders around the images.
The background edging paper was stained with tea.

Library of Congress Cataloging-in-Publication Data

Fradin, Dennis B.
Nicolaus Copernicus : the earth is a planet / by Dennis Brindell Fradin ; illustrated by
Cynthia von Buhler.
p. cm.
Summary: A biography of astronomer Nicolaus Copernicus, who challenged the belief of
his age that Earth was the center of the universe and proved that it is, instead, a planet orbiting the Sun.
ISBN 1-59336-006-1 (hc : alk. paper) -- ISBN 1-59336-007-X (pbk. : alk. paper)
1. Copernicus, Nicolaus, 1473-1543--juvenile literature. 2 Astronomers--Poland--Biography--Juvenile
Literature. [1. Copernicus, Nicolaus, 1473-1543. 2. Astronomers. 3.Scientists.] I. Buhler, Cynthia von, ill.
II. Title.

QB36.C8F73 2003
520'.92--dc22
   [B]   2003056147